# The
# Cat
# Notebook

Running Press
Philadelphia, Pennsylvania

*Who can believe that there is no soul
behind those luminous eyes!*

—THEOPHILE GAUTIER

*With the qualities of cleanliness, discretion, affection, patience, dignity, and courage that cats have, how many of us, I ask you, would be capable of being cats?*

—FERNAND MERY

*It is in the nature of cats to do a certain amount of unescorted roaming.*

—ADLAI STEVENSON

*In the middle of a world
that has always been a bit mad,
the cat walks with confidence.*

—ROSANNE AMBERSON

*The cat is a dilettante in fur.*
—THEOPHILE GAUTIER

*It is with the approach of winter that cats become*
*in a special manner our friends and guests. It is then*
*too that they wear their richest fur and assume*
*an air of sumptuous and delightful opulence.*

—PIERRE LOTI

*Dogs remember faces, cats places.*
—ENGLISH SAYING

*The cat is mighty dignified until the dog comes by.*

—SOUTHERN FOLK SAYING

*The real objection to the great majority of cats is their insufferable air of superiority.*

—P.G. WODEHOUSE

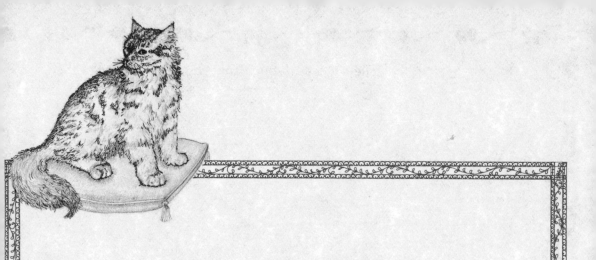

Her function is to sit and be admired.
—GEORGINA STRICKLAND GATES

*The cat sees through shut lids.*
—ENGLISH SAYING

*Cats are rather delicate creatures and they are subject to a good many ailments, but I never heard of one who suffered from insomnia.*

—JOSEPH WOOD KRUTCH

*The trouble with cats is that they've got no tact.*

—P.G. WODEHOUSE

*Cats seem to go on the principle that it never does any harm to ask for what you want.*

—JOSEPH WOOD KRUTCH

*I gave an order to the cat,*
*and the cat gave it to its tail.*
—CHINESE PROVERB

*A kitten is so flexible that she is almost double; the hind parts are equivalent to another kitten with which the forepart plays. She does not discover that her tail belongs to her until you tread on it.*

—HENRY DAVID THOREAU

*No matter how much cats fight, there always seem to be plenty of kittens.*

—ABRAHAM LINCOLN

*A cat with kittens nearly always decides
sooner or later to move them.*

—SIDNEY DENHAM

*Never ask a hungry cat whether he loves you for yourself alone.*

—DR. LOUIS J. CAMUTI

*Honest as the cat when the meat is out of reach.*

—ENGLISH SAYING

*A cat is nobody's fool.*
—HEYWOOD BROUN

He loved books, and when he found one open on the table he would lie down on it, turn over the edges of the leaves with his paw, and, after a while, fall asleep, for all the world as if he had been reading a fashionable novel.

—THEOPHILE GAUTIER

*There was a sound between them. A warm and contented sound like the murmur of giant bees in a hollow tree.*

—STEPHEN VINCENT BENET

*All you have to remember is Rule 1:*
*When in doubt—Wash.*

—PAUL GALLICO

*He shut his eyes while Saha [the cat] kept vigil, watching all the invisible signs that hover over sleeping human beings when the light is put out.*

—COLETTE

*A dog, I have always said, is prose;*
*a cat is a poem.*

—JEAN BURDEN

*At dinner time he would sit in a corner, concentrating, and suddenly they would say, "Time to feed the cat," as if it were their own idea.*

—LILIAN JACKSON BRAUN

*Cats know how to obtain food without labor, shelter
without confinement, and love without penalties.*

—W.L. GEORGE

*Cats always know whether people like or dislike them.*
*They do not always care enough to do anything about it.*

—WINIFRED CARRIERE

*The way to keep a cat is to try to chase it away.*

—ED HOWE

*The cat is utterly sincere.*
—FERNAND MERY

*If you want to be a psychological novelist and write about human beings, the best thing you can do is keep a pair of cats.*

—ALDOUS HUXLEY

*One of the most striking differences between a cat and a lie is that a cat has only nine lives.*

—MARK TWAIN

*The Cat was a creature of absolute convictions,
and his faith in his deductions never varied.*

—MARY E. WILKINS FREEMAN

*Most cats, when they are Out want to be In,*
*and vice versa, and often simultaneously.*

—DR. LOUIS J. CAMUTI

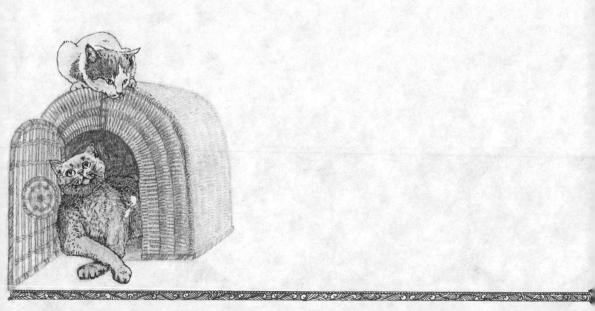

*If he had asked to have the door opened, and was eager to go out, he always went out deliberately. I can see him now, standing on the sill, looking about the sky as if he was thinking whether it were worth while to take an umbrella, until he was near to having his tail shut in.*

—CHARLES DUDLEY WARNER

*A cat is a tiger that is fed by hand.*
—YAKAOKA GENRIN

*Everything that moves serves to interest and amuse a cat.*

—F.A. PARADIS DE MONCRIF

*Cats know not how to pardon.*
—JEAN DE LA FONTAINE

*What's virtue in man can't be vice in a cat.*

—MARY ABIGAIL DODGE

*Kittens believe that all nature is occupied with their diversion.*
—F.A. PARADIS DE MONCRIF

*To please himself only the cat purrs.*
—IRISH PROVERB

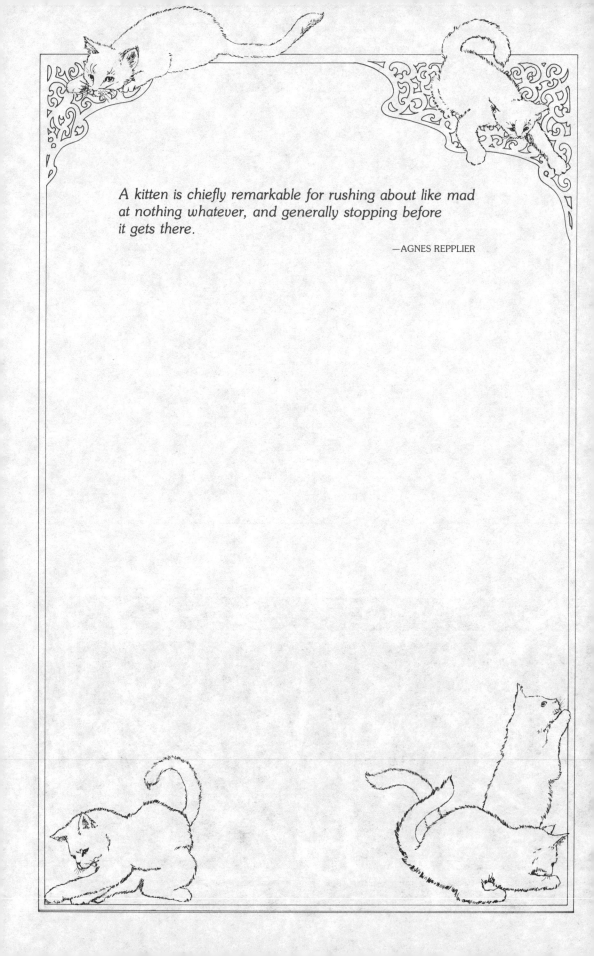

*A kitten is chiefly remarkable for rushing about like mad
at nothing whatever, and generally stopping before
it gets there.*

—AGNES REPPLIER

As a kitten, this cat never slept on the outside of the bed. She waited until I was in it, then she walked all over me, considering possibilities.

—DORIS LESSING

*The cat is the mirror of his human's mind, personality and attitude, just as the dog mirrors his human's physical appearance.*

—WINIFRED CARRIERE

It is a difficult matter to gain the affection of a cat. He is a philosophical, methodical animal, tenacious of his own habits, fond of order and neatness, and disinclined to extravagant sentiment. He will be your friend, if he finds you worthy of friendship, but not your slave.

—THEOPHILE GAUTIER

*With cats one can never be certain.*
—HARTLEY AND JOAN RAMSAY

*Although all cat games have their rules and ritual, these vary with the individual player. The cat, of course, never breaks a rule. If it does not follow precedent, that simply means it has created a new rule and it is up to you to learn it quickly if you want the game to continue.*

—SIDNEY DENHAM

*Cats are admirably designed to be curious.*

—ERIC GURNEY

*Nothing's more playful than a young cat,*
*nor more grave than an old one.*

—THOMAS FULLER

*Somebody once said that a dog looked up to a man
as its superior, that a horse regarded a man
as its equal, and that a cat looked down on him
as its inferior.*

—COMPTON MACKENZIE

The cat seldom interferes with other people's rights.
His intelligence keeps him from doing many
of the fool things that complicate life.

—CARL VAN VECHTEN

*Of all domestic animals the cat is the most expressive. His face is capable of showing a wide range of expressions. His tail is a mirror of his mind. His gracefulness is surpassed only by his agility. And, along with all these, he has a sense of humor.*

—WALTER CHANDOHA

*There is no more intrepid explorer than a kitten.*
—JULES CHAMPFLEURY

*Cats can be very funny, and have the oddest ways of showing they're glad to see you. Rudimace always peed in our shoes.*

—W.H. AUDEN

It is a very inconvenient habit of kittens (Alice had once made the remark) that, whatever you say to them, they always purr.

—LEWIS CARROLL

*Cats will always lie soft.*
—THEOCRITUS

*For me, one of the pleasures of cats' company*
*is their devotion to bodily comfort.*

—COMPTON MACKENZIE

*In many respects, cats are more like men and women than dogs; they have moods, and their nature is complex.*

—HELEN WINSLOW

*The really great thing about cats is their endless variety. One can pick a cat to fit almost any kind of decor, color scheme, income, personality, mood. But under the fur, whatever color it may be, there still lies, essentially unchanged, one of the world's free souls.*

—ERIC GURNEY

Cats find malicious amusement in doing what they know they are not wanted to do, and that with an affectation of innocence that materially aggravates their deliberate offense.

—HELEN WINSLOW

*The cat is never vulgar.*

—CARL VAN VECHTEN

*Watch a cat when it enters a room for the first time. It searches and smells about, it is not quiet for a moment, it trusts nothing until it has examined and made acquaintance with everything.*

—JEAN JACQUES ROUSSEAU

*The cat is, above all things, a dramatist.*
—MARGARET BENSON

*He walked by himself, and all places were alike to him.*
—RUDYARD KIPLING

*Cats do not go for a walk to get somewhere but to explore.*

—SIDNEY DENHAM

*The ideal of calm exists in a sitting cat.*

—JULES REYNARD

*You could never accuse him of idleness,*
*and yet he knew the secret of repose.*

—CHARLES DUDLEY WARNER

*I suspect that many an ailurophobe hates cats only because he feels they are better people than he is—more honest, more secure, more loved, more whatever he is not.*

—WINIFRED CARRIERE

*Cats love one so much—more than they will allow.*
*But they have so much wisdom they keep it to themselves.*

—MARY WILKINS

*If I called her she would pretend not to hear,
but would come a few moments later when
it could appear that she had thought of
doing so first.*

—ARTHUR WEIGALL

Tobermory looked squarely at her for a moment and then fixed his gaze serenely on the middle distance. It was obvious that boring questions lay outside his scheme of life.

—SAKI

She walks her chosen path by our side;
but our ways are not her ways, our
influence does not remotely reach her.

—AGNES REPPLIER

*It is as easy to hold quicksilver between your finger and thumb as to keep a cat who means to escape.*

—ANDREW LANG

*If a fish is the movement of water embodied, given shape, then a cat is a diagram and pattern of subtle air.*

—DORIS LESSING

*He lives in the half-lights in secret places,
free and alone — this mysterious little-great
being whom his mistress calls "My cat."*

—MARGARET BENSON

*The most domesticated of cats somehow contrives to lead an outside life of its own.*

—KATHARINE BRIGGS

The cat lives alone, has no need of society, obeys only when she pleases, pretends to sleep that she may see the more clearly, and scratches everything on which she can lay her paw.

—FRANCOIS RENE DE CHATEAUBRIAND

*There is nothing so lowering to one's self-esteem
as the affectionate contempt of a beloved cat.*

—AGNES REPPLIER

*Nobody who is not prepared to spoil cats will get from them the reward they are able to give to those who do spoil them.*

—COMPTON MACKENZIE

*No tame animal has lost less of its native dignity
or maintained more of its ancient reserve.
The domestic cat might rebel tomorrow.*

—WILLIAM CONWAY

*I could half persuade myself that the word felonious
is derived from the feline temper.*

—ROBERT SOUTHEY

*One reason we admire cats is for their proficiency in one-upmanship. They always seem to come out on top, no matter what they are doing—or pretend they do.*

—BARBARA WEBSTER

*The smart cat doesn't let on that he is.*

—H.G. FROMMER

*The cat is the only animal without visible means of support who still manages to find a living in the city.*

—CARL VAN VECHTEN

*I love in the cat that independent and most ungrateful
temper which prevents it from attaching itself to
anyone; the indifference with which it passes from
the salon to the housetop.*

—FRANCOIS RENE DE CHATEAUBRIAND

*I called my cat William because no shorter name fits the dignity of his character. Poor old man, he has fits now, so I call him Fitz-William.*

—JOSH BILLINGS

*If man could be crossed with the cat, it would improve man
but deteriorate the cat.*

—MARK TWAIN

*The only mystery about the cat is why it ever decided to become a domestic animal.*

—COMPTON MACKENZIE

*The cat is the only animal which accepts the comforts but rejects the bondage of domesticity.*

—GEORGES LOUIS LECLERC DE BUFFON

*To understand a cat, you must realize
that he has his own gifts, his own
viewpoint, even his own morality.*

—LILIAN JACKSON BRAUN

*Cats are a mysterious kind of folk.*
*There is more passing in their minds*
*than we are aware of.*

—SIR WALTER SCOTT